J921
FER

George Ferris' Grand Idea

THE FERRIS WHEEL

by Jenna Glatzer

illustrated by
Stephanie Dominguez

PICTURE WINDOW BOOKS
a capstone imprint

George Washington Gale Ferris Jr. had some thinking to do. And when he needed to think, he liked to sit in front of the big waterwheel near his home. "What can I do that's important?" he wondered.

George lived on his parents' ranch in Nevada. He dreamed of doing something big with his life. But when you're one of 10 children, it can be hard to stand out.

In the late 1870s, George decided to become a civil engineer. He went to college in New York and designed all kinds of things. He was good at his work. Soon he was put in charge of building tunnels and bridges. It was very dangerous, stressful work, but George was proud to help people travel safely.

Years later, in early 1892, an exciting announcement was made. The United States would host the 1893 World's Fair in Chicago, Illinois. At each World's Fair, people from many nations showed off their finest inventions, artwork, and products. Daniel Burnham, director of the Chicago fair, challenged engineers to create a centerpiece. He wanted something "novel, original, daring, and unique."

"The star of the show at the last World's Fair in Paris was the Eiffel Tower," Burnham said. "I want an American to do something even greater than that!"

Greater than the Eiffel Tower? What a challenge! Many engineers drew *their* ideas for towers. George had a better idea, though. He imagined something not only giant, but fun too. He pictured a huge contraption that looked like a bicycle wheel. It would take people on an amazing ride high up into the sky. How high? Try 265 feet (81 meters). About as tall as a skyscraper!

"Your wheel is so flimsy it will collapse, and even if it doesn't, the public will be afraid to ride in it," said Burnham.

But George was a good salesman. He promised Burnham that his wheel would not fall down. He said he would raise enough money to build it himself. Finally, after several weeks, Burnham said yes to George's idea—even if he did think it was crazy.

Then came the hard part. George had to raise almost $400,000 to buy materials and hire workers. He went to the bank for a loan to build his "Observation Wheel."

"Are you kidding? There must be wheels in your head!" the banker said.

George heard the same thing at the next bank and the next.

"I will not give up," George thought. He explained his idea to investors and asked them to help him make history. Many of them loaned him money. They also told him he should name his invention the Ferris Wheel.

George had just a few months to build his giant wheel. He hired nine steel mills to make all the steel he would need—enough to fill 150 train cars. Then he hired workers to dig eight huge holes in the ground and fill them with concrete. The wheel needed a strong base so it wouldn't fall over—like a tall tree needs strong roots. But there was a big problem: It was winter in Chicago. The ground was frozen solid.

15

While temperatures dived below zero, workers struggled to dig the holes. It took a long time, but the men did it. And then the unthinkable happened. They hit quicksand! Workers scrambled to dig out all the quicksand. They didn't want it to swallow up the concrete they were about to pour.

That wasn't the end of George's troubles. When workers tried to pour the concrete, it quickly froze! George had to pipe steam into the holes. The heat helped the concrete harden slowly, in the proper way.

The World's Fair opened in Chicago on May 1, 1893, but the Ferris Wheel wasn't ready. There was still more work to be done. Burnham was angry.

"Finish that wheel!" he boomed.

George pushed his men to work faster. They still needed to finish the gondolas. Instead of carrying passengers in open seats, like today's Ferris wheels, George's wheel used glass-windowed gondolas. Each of the 36 cabins could hold up to 60 passengers. When all the gondolas were full, more than 2,000 people could ride at once. The cabins even had tables in the middle for food and drinks.

Finally, on June 11, the Ferris Wheel was ready for a test run. It had taken six months to build. Even though many people were scared it would crash, George's wife, Margaret, was brave. She gladly volunteered to be one of the first passengers. It took 20 minutes for the wheel to make two full revolutions, the length of the ride. Margaret was happy that her husband's dream had come true.

"I have always believed in you," she told him later. She gave him a golden whistle to blow to signal that the Ferris Wheel was officially open.

It cost 50 cents for a ticket to the World's Fair (about $12 today) and an extra 50 cents to ride the Ferris Wheel. Not everyone could afford the extra money, so many people just enjoyed watching. It was quite a sight!

"I leave it to you, ladies and gentlemen, to say if the wheels are still in my head," George said to the crowd.

All kinds of people loved riding the Ferris Wheel. Couples even wanted to get married on it. By the time the Fair closed in November, nearly 1.5 million tickets had been sold. It was a huge success!

The wish George had made when he was a boy came true: He did something important. His marvelous wheel became famous and has made people happy all around the world. Almost every amusement park now has a Ferris wheel.

Afterword

After the 1893 World's Fair was over, it was very hard to move the Ferris Wheel. It weighed more than 2 million pounds (907 metric tons)—about the weight of 520 elephants! It was taken apart, moved nearby, and then moved to another fair in Louisiana in 1904. But it was not as popular as it had been before. By then many copycat Ferris wheels had been made, and people weren't as amazed by George's wheel anymore.

The original Ferris Wheel was blown up with 100 sticks of dynamite in May 1906.

Today the tallest Ferris wheel in the world is in Las Vegas, Nevada. It stands 550 feet (168 m) tall—more than twice the height of George's original wheel.

George Ferris, circa 1893

Las Vegas High Roller

Glossary

centerpiece—the main focus or attraction

collapse—to fall down suddenly

contraption—a machine or device that may look complicated

Eiffel Tower—a tall iron tower in Paris, France, designed by Gustave Eiffel

flimsy—without strength

gondola—a type of cabin that carries people above the ground

investor—someone who provides money for a project in return for a share in the profits

loan—money that is borrowed with a plan to pay it back

novel—new and different

observation—the act of carefully looking

revolution—one complete turn all the way around

site—the position or location of something

transport—to move or carry something or someone from one place to another

unthinkable—something that is beyond what is reasonable or likely

Critical Thinking Using the Common Core

1. The leader of the fair, Daniel Burnham, asked engineers to create something "novel, original, daring, and unique." Describe how the Ferris Wheel met all of these goals. **[Key Ideas and Details]**

2. Name the many problems George ran into while trying to build his Ferris Wheel. Then describe how he solved each of them. **[Key Ideas and Details]**

3. What did the banker mean when he said that George must have wheels in his head? Later, what did George mean when he said, "I leave it to you, ladies and gentlemen, to say if the wheels are still in my head"? **[Craft and Structure]**

Read More

Davis, Kathryn G. *Mr. Ferris and His Wheel.* Boston: Houghton Mifflin Harcourt, 2014.

Lowell, Barbara. *George Ferris, What a Wheel.* Penguin Core Concepts. New York: Grosset & Dunlap, 2014.

Sneed, Dani. *The Man Who Invented the Ferris Wheel: The Genius of George Ferris.* Genius Inventors and Their Great Ideas. Berkeley Heights, N.J.: Enslow Publishers, 2013.

Internet Sites

FactHound offers a safe, fun way to find Internet sites related to this book. All of the sites on FactHound have been researched by our staff.

Here's all you do:

Visit *www.facthound.com*

Type in this code: 9781479571352

Super-cool stuff! Check out projects, games and lots more at **www.capstonekids.com**

Look for all the books in the series:

Special thanks to our adviser for his expertise:
Terry Flaherty, PhD, Professor of English
Minnesota State University, Mankato

Editor: Jill Kalz
Designer: Lori Bye
Creative Director: Nathan Gassman
Production Specialist: Laura Manthe
The illustrations in this book were created digitally.

Picture Window Books are published by Capstone,
1710 Roe Crest Drive, North Mankato, Minnesota 56003
www.capstonepub.com

Shutterstock/Aneese, 29; Wikimedia/Tohma,
Vierundnull, 29 (top right)

Library of Congress Cataloging-in-Publication Data
Glatzer, Jenna.
  George Ferris' grand idea : the Ferris wheel / by Jenna Glatzer.
     pages cm. — (Picture Window Books. The Story Behind the Name.)
  Includes bibliographical references and index.
  Summary: "Discusses George Ferris' invention of the Ferris Wheel
and the man behind it, including the idea, the obstacles, and the
eventual success"—Provided by publisher.
  ISBN 978-1-4795-7135-2 (library binding)
  ISBN 978-1-4795-7161-1 (paper over board)
  ISBN 978-1-4795-7165-9 (paperback)
  ISBN 978-1-4795-7177-2 (eBook PDF)
1. Ferris, George Washington Gale, 1859–1896—Juvenile literature. 2.
Structural engineers—United States—Biography—Juvenile literature.
3. Civil engineers—United States—Biography—Juvenile literature. 4.
Inventors—United States—Biography—Juvenile literature. 5. Ferris
wheels—History—Juvenile literature. I. Title
TA140.F455G53 2016
791.06'80284—dc23   2014049209

Printed in the United States of America
in North Mankato, Minnesota.
032015   008823CGF15